A IS FOR ANIMALS

the ABC Rhyming Book

Learn your ABCs in a fun rhyme
using animal names.

Written by **H.A. Spires**
Illustrated by **Tatiana Minina**

© Hugh Spires, 2020

About the Author:

Hugh Spires, Jr. is a father, grandfather and lawyer who makes humor part of his daily routine. He grew up in a small town in south Arkansas and learned to entertain himself (and sometimes others) by telling jokes, performing magic tricks, and riding his unicycle. Fifty years later, he still has a joke ready or funny story to tell.

To my children Bianca and Tripp and grandson Audie for keeping me young at heart and giving me an excuse to be silly.

A is for Anteater

B is for Bull

C is for caterpillar who wakes up for school.

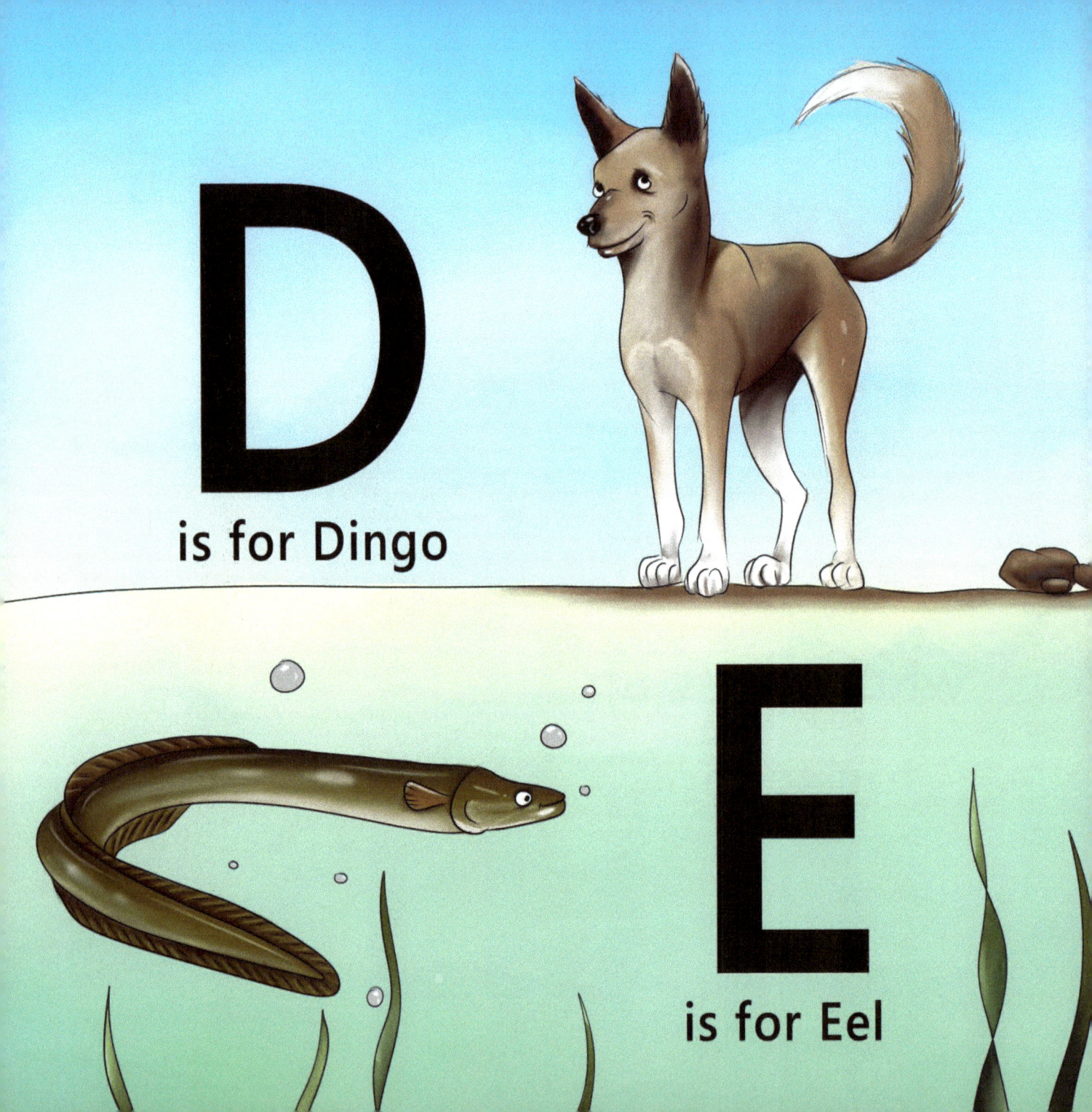

F

is for Flamingo,
who often
stand still.

G
is for Gorilla

H
is for Horse

M
is for Manatee

N

is for Newt

O

is for Orangutan,
who likes his
new suit.

R

is for Racoon,
who has a
striped tail.

S
is for Scorpion

T
is for Tang

U

is for Unicorn,
that exists
in our brain.

is for X-ray Tetra,
with a see
through tail.

Y
is for Yellow
Eyed Penguin

Z is for Zorse
It is a both a zebra
and a horse . . .
of course.